IMAGES
of America

BRANCHBURG
AND THE RIVER TOWNS OF
BURNT MILLS, NORTH BRANCH,
NORTH BRANCH DEPOT, SOUTH BRANCH,
AND NESHANIC STATION

Shadow Lawn, the great Victorian mansion of Judge John G. Schenck, was built in 1858 when the area of Neshanic Station was his farm, and the railroads had not yet come to this part of town. (Branchburg Historic Preservation Commission.)

IMAGES
of America

BRANCHBURG

AND THE RIVER TOWNS OF
BURNT MILLS, NORTH BRANCH,
NORTH BRANCH DEPOT, SOUTH BRANCH,
AND NESHANIC STATION

William A. Schleicher, Susan J. Winter, and Robert Bouwman

ARCADIA

ISBN 0-7524-0239-0

Published by Arcadia Publishing,
an imprint of the Chalford Publishing Corporation
One Washington Center, Dover, New Hampshire 03820
Printed in Great Britain

Library of Congress Cataloging-in-Publication Data applied for

A detail of the front door from the White Oak Tavern, showing its hand-wrought, eighteenth-century Suffolk latch. The door, which is all that remains of the old stage coach inn, now belongs to the Branchburg Historical Society. The first township committee meeting was held at this tavern, which was then operated by Isaac "Shifty Ike" Hall, on April 14, 1845. We were unable to find a picture of the tavern to include in this book. Do you know where we can find one? (Branchburg Historical Society.)

Contents

Acknowledgments

To the many people who shared their treasured photographs and stories with us, we extend our heartfelt thanks: George William (Bill) Amerman; Ray Bateman; Wilma Blaufuss; Sergeant Wayne Daniels, or whoever he is today; the Field family; Robert Gurerl; Jack Gentempo; George Greenaway; Lee Hamilton; Marie Harwitt; Fred Heilich; George Hunter; Charles Karbowski; Carol Philhower; Eric Smith; Lorraine and Marilyn Solberg; Grace Staats; Dorothy Stratford; and Walter Studdiford.

We would also like to thank the following organizations for giving us access to their archives: The Branchburg Historical Society; The Branchburg Historic Preservation Commission; The Clarence Dillon Memorial Library; The Gardner Sage Memorial Library of the New Brunswick Theological Seminary; The Neshanic Station Historical Society; Rutgers University, Alexander Library, Special Collection; The Somerset County Historical Society; The Somerset County Library; and the Somerville Fireman's Museum.

Finally, we would like to thank our spouses, Dorothy, Norm, and Rita, for tolerating our eccentric ways, permitting the distractions, and abiding the mess.

"Good reader, blame not the wrytter, for that that is myssing in this booke is not his faulte. What he hath founde—as nere as possybell he could—he hath set down."

—from an English Parish Register, 1582.

Introduction

Traces of the past remain to testify of those who've gone before. The first settlers of the region were the Lenni Lenape, who built their lodges under a towering canopy of oaks along the river over 9,000 years before the first European settlers arrived. The name "Lenni Lenape," meaning "Original People," was given to them by the more "come lately" Indians who, when they arrived millennia ago, found the Lenape already here. For 2,000 years before the building of the great pyramids of Egypt, the Lenape hunted our forests and fished our rivers. "Tucca-Ramma-Hacking," which means "meeting place of the waters," was what they called the place where today Old York Road crosses into Bradley Gardens. This area, where the north and south branches of the Raritan River flow together, was a meeting place for the Indians, not only because of the transportation the river provided but also because it was a crossing point of two ancient Indian trails. One led from Easton and beyond, to Sandy Hook, and the other meandered from Port Jarvis to Little Egg Harbor. Many tribes peacefully passed this way on their nomadic journeys to the great oyster fields of the shore, or back to the hunting grounds of the beautiful blue mountains. Tucca-Ramma-Hacking remained a permanent settlement. It was a place of trade. Arrow heads and stone implements were manufactured here and traded for ones made of stone native to different regions, or beads fashioned from sea shells. Here the banks of the river from below Bound Brook to above Neshanic were cleared and cultivated, providing food for locals and travelers. Great collections of arrow heads and other stone implements have been accumulated near the confluence of the Raritan River, attesting to the lengthy tenure of the Indians.

Hendrick Corson Vroom, a kind of a Dutch Daniel Boone, established a trading post at Tucca-Ramma-Hacking by 1680 to trade European manufactured goods for furs. Here he was joined by Thomas Holland and his son Christian. They learned the language of the Lenape and bought land from them. Vroom settled on a tract beginning at the river and running on the north side of what is now Old York Road. Thomas Holland bought the land south of the road along the river from the confluence, to the stream the Indians called "Wiseconsie." Between 1684 and 1686, on commission from Governor Lawrie, Hendrick Vroom laid out the Old York Road along the ancient Indian trails. The Dutch called this first official road in Somerset County the "Road up Raritan." To the English it was the "Great Road," or the "King's Highway," though it was barely wide enough for a wagon to pass. When Andrew Hamilton, with his his great curly wig flowing over his shoulders, arrived to purchase land for the Lords' proprietors of East Jersey in 1685, it was Holland and Vroom who interpreted for him. Think of

Hendrick Vroom when you travel the Old York Road, and Thomas Holland when you pass Holland's Brook, the stream the Indians called "Wiseconnsie."

Perhaps our oldest tree is the giant oak towering beside the Vosseller burying ground, just a short distance from the grave of Captain George Vroom. Or perhaps it could be one of the great sycamores along the river banks. What history these silent sentinels have witnessed. Well over two hundred years in age, yet they never knew the Indians. Our forefathers cleared the land for cultivation, and to build and heat their homes. The great stand of oak and ash known as "Bowman's Woods" is the eighteenth-century woodlot of Colonel Abraham Ten Eyck. Many old Dutch barns have giant anchor beams, some of which measure 20 inches by 30 inches by over 40 feet, made out of trees that knew the Indians.

Red and green coaches with gold trim and brass fittings once traveled the Old York Road from New York to Philadelphia. Coachmen in buckskin breeches, high boots, and red vests wore silk hats with gold bands and the brims turned up at the sides. The coach guard blew his horn from a half mile distant as they approached a village. People from nearby came running to hear what news they brought from the outside, and to get their mail. The driver would rein-in the horses in front of the tavern with his foot on the brake lever. The tavern keeper would appear at the door and offer the coachmen a snappy salute, to which the driver would respond with his whip at present arms. Then everyone would adjourn to the bar for some refreshment. The White Oak Tavern stood on the north side of the Old York Road just east of Stony Brook Road. For two centuries it served the stage coaches until the railroads and automobiles put them out of business. It was there that the first township committee meeting was held in 1845 when Issac "Shifty Ike" Hall was the proprietor. It was too much gunpowder they say, set in the hollow of the old white oak by some politician to celebrate an election victory, that blew up the tavern's namesake. And it was demolition by neglect that finally brought down the old tavern early in this century. All that remains is the front door, which belongs to the Branchburg Historical Society, and the name of White Oak Park. In Centerville, the Swift Sure Stage Coach Barn can still be seen.

Since the invention of the camera, we've had many more images to testify about the past, like the coming of the railroads, and the first automobiles. Around the turn of the century, general store owners like J.E. Glaser in North Branch Depot, and J. Bradford Opie in Neshanic Station, sold a line of postcards featuring photographs of local scenes. Now and then they turn up in antique shops and flea markets. Quite a few have found their way into this book, along with many treasured family photographs, stored away for years in local attics. Some record the presence of famous people, while others depict everyday life in a simpler age. Perhaps you will be surprised to learn how the boys in one school could fish if the teacher wasn't watching. Perhaps you'll even see a picture of your own house! Enjoy a trip down memory lane; then, if you have any old photographs of Branchburg that aren't in this book, show them to us. We would love to see them.

One

Tucca-Ramma-Hacking: The Indian Camp Grounds

Prior to the arrival of European settlers, American Indians hunted and fished in the local forests and streams. For 9,000 years the confluence of the North and South Branches of the Raritan River was a favorite campground. They called this place "Tucca-Ramma-Hacking," which meant "meeting place of the waters." For the Indians, the canoe was an important form of transportation. In addition to the waterways, two important Indian trails also intersected at this site. One led from Easton Pennsylvania to Sandy Hook, and the other led from Port Jervis, New York, to Little Egg Harbor. This double intersection of rivers and trails caused this to become one of the Indians, most vital trading centers. When the Dutch and English settlers arrived, they found the banks of the Raritan River cleared and cultivated from below Bound Brook to past Neshanic. (Branchburg Historical Society.)

There is much of archeological interest in the remains of this habitation, which includes evidence of the manufacture of arrow heads and other stone implements. One of the largest collections of stone implements ever assembled in the state was gathered in the area of the confluence. (Somerset County Historical Society.)

Dutch settler Hendrick Corson Vroom established an Indian Trading Post at Tucca-Ramma-Hacking around 1680, buying land north of Old York Road directly from the Indians. He primarily traded European manufactured goods, like knives and axes, for furs. About this same time Thomas Holland purchased 250 acres of land directly from the Indians. His land started at the confluence of the Raritan Rivers, and ran along the South Branch as far as the brook that the Indians called "Wiseconsie," which since that time has been known as Holland's Brook. When the English proprietors came to buy land in Branchburg from the Indians, Hendrick Vroom and Thomas Holland were already here, and acted as interpreters.

Two
The Colonial Period and the American Revolution

Captain Andrew Hamilton, a merchant from Edinburgh, Scotland, negotiated the purchase of land in Branchburg from the Indians beginning in 1685, using the Dutch settlers Thomas Holland and Hendrick Vroom as interpreters. He was appointed deputy governor of East Jersey in 1687 under Lord Neil Campbell. He later became governor of East and West Jersey, and deputy governor of Pennsylvania. He bought three tracts of land in Branchburg as an investor, but never settled here.

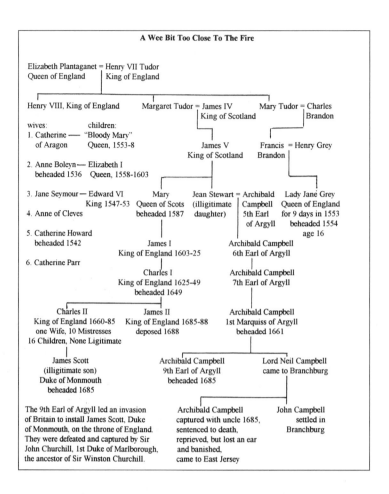

A Wee Bit Too Close To The Fire

Elizabeth Plantaganet = Henry VII Tudor
Queen of England / King of England

Henry VIII, King of England

wives: / children:
1. Catherine —— "Bloody Mary"
   of Aragon / Queen, 1553-8

2. Anne Boleyn —— Elizabeth I
   beheaded 1536 / Queen, 1558-1603

3. Jane Seymour —— Edward VI
   King 1547-53
4. Anne of Cleves

5. Catherine Howard
   beheaded 1542

6. Catherine Parr

Margaret Tudor = James IV
King of Scotland

James V
King of Scotland

Mary Tudor = Charles
Brandon

Francis = Henry Grey
Brandon

Mary / Jean Stewart = Archibald / Lady Jane Grey
Queen of Scots / (illigitimate / Campbell / Queen of England
beheaded 1587 / daughter) / 5th Earl / for 9 days in 1553
of Argyll / beheaded 1554
age 16

James I
King of England 1603-25

Charles I
King of England 1625-49
beheaded 1649

Archibald Campbell
6th Earl of Argyll

Archibald Campbell
7th Earl of Argyll

Charles II
King of England 1660-85
one Wife, 10 Mistresses
16 Children, None Ligitimate

James II
King of England 1685-88
deposed 1688

Archibald Campbell
1st Marquiss of Argyll
beheaded 1661

James Scott
(illigitimate son)
Duke of Monmouth
beheaded 1685

Archibald Campbell
9th Earl of Argyll
beheaded 1685

Lord Neil Campbell
came to Branchburg

The 9th Earl of Argyll led an invasion
of Britain to install James Scott, Duke
of Monmouth, on the throne of England.
They were defeated and captured by Sir
John Churchill, 1st Duke of Marlborough,
the ancestor of Sir Winston Churchill.

Archibald Campbell
captured with uncle 1685,
sentenced to death,
reprieved, but lost an ear
and banished,
came to East Jersey

John Campbell
settled in
Branchburg

The Lords' proprietors of East Jersey and the first land grants. In the late 1600s, James Duke of York, brother of King Charles II of England, granted patents for all the land in New Jersey, and the right to form a government, to two groups of proprietors. West Jersey was granted to Quakers seeking religious freedom. The East Jersey proprietors were mostly Scots seeking wealth. Almost all the land in Branchburg was first granted in large tracts to the individual proprietors themselves. The map on the facing page shows the location and extent of those grants. Although a few of them made an effort to establish plantations, most were purely speculators, and all had sold their land to the first real settlers within a few years. A number of them were very wealthy and influential Scots at a time when the King of England was a Stuart from the Royal Scottish line. During the period when the first land grants were being made in Branchburg, one of the major issues to be facing the proprietors was the establishment of a line to separate the two provinces. One line that was proposed would have been drawn from Little Egg Harbor directly through what is now Somerville. But when the dust settled, Governors Cox and Barclay agreed on September 5, 1688, that the line should run "straight from Little Egg Harbor to the most westerly corner of John Dobie's Plantation as it stands on the South Branch of the Raritan River . . . thence to run along the back of the adjoining Plantations . . ." Part of the reason for the acceptance of this line was that a more easterly alternative would have invalidated the land grants of some very influential Scots proprietors. Whether the line was drawn to validate the land grants, or the land grants were made to influence the line, the net effect was to give the East Jersey proprietors hundreds of thousands more acres to sell in a triangle of land from Somerville to Branchburg and extending all the way to Little Egg Harbor.

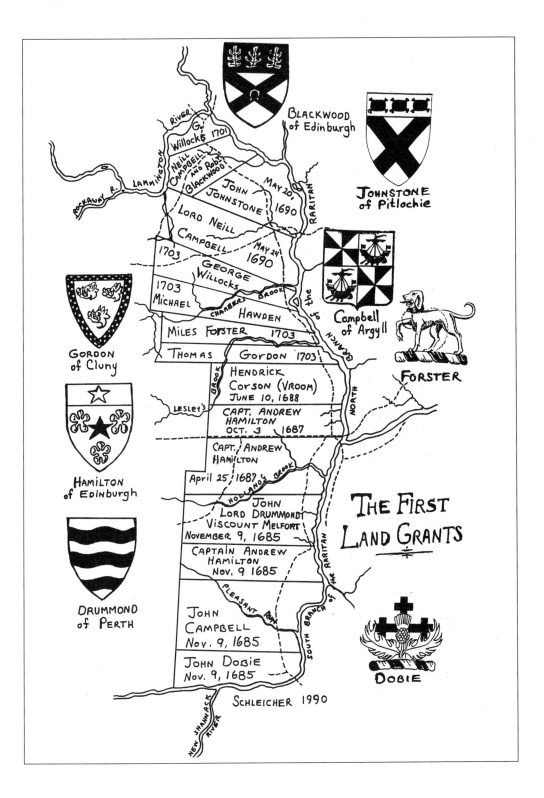

BLACKWOOD of Edinburgh

JOHNSTONE of Pitlochie

GORDON of Cluny

HAMILTON of Edinburgh

DRUMMOND of Perth

Campbell of Argyll

FORSTER

THE FIRST LAND GRANTS

DOBIE

G. Willocks 1701

Neill Campbell and Robt Blackwood

JOHN JOHNSTONE MAY 20, 1690

LORD NEILL CAMPBELL MAY 24 1690

1703

GEORGE Willocks 1703

Michael Hawden

Miles Forster 1703

THOMAS Gordon 1703

HENDRICK CORSON (VROOM) JUNE 10, 1688

CAPT. ANDREW HAMILTON OCT. 3 1687

LESLEY'S

CAPT. ANDREW HAMILTON April 25, 1687

JOHN LORD DRUMMOND VISCOUNT MELFORT November 9, 1685

CAPTAIN ANDREW HAMILTON Nov. 9 1685

JOHN CAMPBELL Nov. 9, 1685

JOHN DOBIE Nov. 9, 1685

LAMMINGTON RIVER

ROCKAWAY R.

RARITAN

CHAMBERS BROOK

the No. BRANCH

NORTH

HOLLANDS BROOK

PLEASANT RUN

SOUTH BRANCH of the RARITAN

NEW SHANNACK RIVER

SCHLEICHER 1990

13

Between 1684 and 1686 Hendrick Corson Vroom laid out Old York Road along ancient Indian trails. At that time it was called the "Road up Raritan" by the Dutch, and the "Great Road," or the "King's Highway," by the English. The first bridge built in Somerset County was the one that crossed the North Branch at the confluence. Later another bridge was built across the confluence to Hillsborough. That part of town then became known as "Two Bridges." During the American Revolution, a company of militia guarded the two bridges, which were considered a vital link and a fall-back route for Washington's army. The bridge to Hillsborough was abandoned after a covered bridge was built to South Branch at Studdiford Road in 1835.

The Indian trails were footpaths only wide enough for a man on foot or on horseback to traverse. The English and Dutch widened them enough so that wagons could get through. During the American Revolution this proved to be a disadvantage to the British. It was only possible to march an army one column (four men) wide. When Lord Howe wanted to move his troops from New Brunswick to Philadelphia in June 1777, the 20,000 men would have formed a column 9 miles long. With supply wagons and stragglers, the line could easily have reached 12 miles. Under those circumstances his men would have suffered enormous losses from the harassment of local militias and Washington's army every step of the way. To avoid this, Howe moved part of his army to Somerset Courthouse (Millstone) in an attempt to lure Washington (at Camp Middlebrook) into a fight. If Howe could defeat Washington in the open field, then he would be free to move his army at will. Washington avoided a fight on his adversary's terms and General Howe was forced to transport his men by ship at much greater cost and loss of time. The following summer General Clinton was not so smart; he attempted to move the army back to New York across New Jersey, suffering terrible losses along the roads and a humiliating defeat in the Battle of Monmouth, the largest engagement of the war.

This is a picture of Old York Road, which Washington traveled on. It lies just west of the Van Vechten House in Bridgewater (which was General Green's headquarters while Washington was at the Wallace House). During the 1800s the course of Old York Road was changed in this area, leaving this section looking just like the entire Old York Road looked from in the early colonial period until the advent of the automobile. During wet weather, wagon wheels turned the road to a sea of mud. (Branchburg Historical Society.)

14

In the old days roads followed property lines, making square corners around farmer's fields. The original alignment of Readington Road has changed between Narraganset Drive and Dow Place. Going north from Narraganset, just before going down the hill, this trail leading off to the right is the original Readington Road. When it reaches the crest of the hill above Leslie's Brook, it turns sharply to the left and crosses the current alignment. (Branchburg Historical Society.)

Old Readington Road continued down what is now a private driveway along the banks of Leslie's Brook. About 500 feet down the drive, Readington Road dog-legged to the right, crossed a cement bridge (the remains of which can still be seen), and reentered the current alignment of Readington Road at Dow Place. At one time this was the Dow farm, and the farmhouse was located near the old bridge. (Branchburg Historical Society.)

Old grave stones displaying the beautiful work of local carvers may be seen in the several family plots that dot the countryside. (Branchburg Historical Society.)

The 1725 Jacob Ten Eyck House. In 1700, Mathias Ten Eyck bought 500 acres of land from John Johnstone. In 1720 he deeded the land to his son Jacob, who built a one-and-a-half-story house on it. The family lived downstairs, and the upstairs was used to store grain. Jacob served in the French and Indian War. His son, Jacob II, was captain of the North Branch militia during the Revolutionary War. After the war he added the second story making it the way it appears today. (Branchburg Historical Society.)

A deed dated October 20, 1720, conveying property in North Branch from Mathias Ten Eyck to his son Jacob, who built the house on the facing page. (Rutgers Special Collection.)

An old Dutch barn on the county land in Branchburg. One December night in 1753, Jacob Van Nest arrived home and dismounted from his horse in front of a barn like this. His slave, thinking that Van Nest had stolen some of his tobacco, was waiting inside the door. Taking an ax, the slave struck down Van Nest and killed him. The body was discovered and suspicion fell upon the slave when he was found to be in possession of some of his master's personal property. (Branchburg Historical Society.)

The slave was taken to the county seat at Millstone for trial. He was convicted and sentenced to death by being burned at the stake. On the day of the execution, many slaves of the region were brought to witness the event. The slaves were formed into a large circle around the condemned with their owners forming an outer circle. Sheriff Van Doren, with his sword drawn, rode his horse between the spectators and the condemned to maintain order. (Branchburg Historical Society.)

This indenture apprenticed George Van Nest, the orphaned son of Jacob Van Nest, to become a carpenter. The apprenticeship also provided a home until he grew up. (Rutgers Special Collection.)

Riverbrook Farm. The oldest part of this house is the first floor on the right which was built about 1750. At that time there was outside cellar access, and cows were kept in the cellar. The center section was built in 1837. Between 1940 and 1946 the Reverend Dr. and Mrs. Hyatt lived here and built the addition and garage on the left. The Hyatts were heirs of the Singer family fortune and came here to escape what they felt to be an imminent German invasion. (George Hunter.)

Riverbrook Farm about the turn of the century when it belonged to the Housel family. The branch of the road passing by the house permitted a horse and wagon to come gently around the hill instead of going directly up Old York Road from the river. For a fee there were teams of horses available at the river to help pull a wagon up the hill. These teams were used by the Swift Sure Stage Coach Line, but a local farmer was likely to avoid the expense by going around the hill. (George Hunter.)

This house on Old York Road, owned by the Cooley family, was built in the eighteenth century. (Branchburg Historical Society.)

"Ridge to River Farm." The earliest part of this house was built about 1770 by the Ten Eyck family. (Branchburg Historical Society.)

The first part of this house was built in the eighteenth century. On May 11, 1813, it was purchased by John and Joanna Liddle from Philip Herder along with 200 acres. John Liddle expanded the house in 1814. Today the house, which lies on Lamington Road, belongs to Raritan Valley Community College and was used until recently as a home for the college president. This photograph was taken in 1950. (From *A Genealogy of the Little Family of Somerset County* by Robert Van Pelt.)

The barns on the Little homestead on Lamington Road. Note the rare Dutch barn with the stone first level. These outbuildings were demolished when Raritan Valley Community College acquired the property. (From *A Genealogy of the Little Family of Somerset County* by Robert Van Pelt.)

The Van Doren House on Lehigh Road about 2 miles west of Neshanic Station. The original four-room home on the right was built by Christianus Van Doren about 1785. His grandson, Abraham Van Doren, added the Federal-style brick main part of the house in 1823. (Branchburg Historical Society.)

The Staats House on Harlan School Road is an eighteenth-century home. (Grace Staats.)

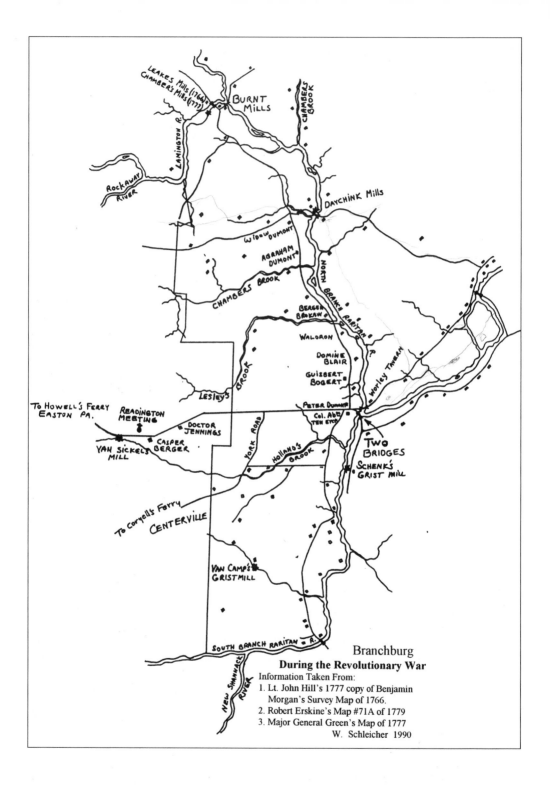

Leakes Mills (1764)
Chamber's Mills (1777)
BURNT MILLS
CHAMBERS BROOK
LAMINGTON R.
ROCKAWAY RIVER
DAYCHINK MILLS
WIDOW DUMONT
ABRAHAM DUMONT
CHAMBERS BROOK
NORTH BRANCH RARITAN
BERGER BROKAW
WALDRON
DOMINE BLAIR
GUISBERT BOGERT
WORLEY TAVERN
LESLEY'S BROOK
PETER DUMONT
Col. Abr. TEN EYCK
TWO BRIDGES
To HOWELL'S FERRY EASTON PA.
READINGTON MEETING
DOCTOR JENNINGS
CASPER BERGER
YAN SICKELS MILL
YORK ROAD
HOLLAND'S BROOK
SCHENK'S GRIST MILL
To Coryell's Ferry
CENTERVILLE
VAN CAMP'S GRISTMILL
SOUTH BRANCH RARITAN R.
NEW SHANNACK RIVER

Branchburg
During the Revolutionary War
Information Taken From:
1. Lt. John Hill's 1777 copy of Benjamin
   Morgan's Survey Map of 1766.
2. Robert Erskine's Map #71A of 1779
3. Major General Green's Map of 1777
   W. Schleicher 1990

During the Revolutionary War period, loyalties and sentiment were not uniformly felt throughout New Jersey. Somerset County was strongly patriotic in the American cause, while there were large numbers of loyalists in Hunterdon County. In 1775, the Provisional Congress and Council of Safety passed a bill directing each township to raise a militia of all men between the edges of sixteen and fifty.

At that time, Branchburg was part of the Township of Bridgewater. The Bridgewater Township Committee named Jacob Ten Eyck, of North Branch, Captain of the militia company drawn from the northern part of Branchburg and parts of Bridgewater. Another company was formed at Two Bridges (where Old York Road crosses the Raritan) under Colonel Abraham Ten Eyck. Men from the southern part of Branchburg joined the "Shannick Company" in Hillsborough.

Whenever the British were in New Jersey, the Branchburg militia (who were also called minutemen) posted guard duty at Two Bridges and other points where the river could be crossed. On December 8, 1776, several hundred loyalists tried to make their way from their homes in Lebanon Township, Hunterdon County, to join the British in New Brunswick. The main road—and most direct route—was the Great Road from Easton, part of which today is Readington Road from the village of Readington, becoming Dreahook and then the Old York Road, and crossing the river at Two Bridges. The alarm was sounded by Dr. Jennings, who lived along the Great Road east of the Readington Reformed Church. The Branchburg militia was called out to intercept the loyalists. Captain Lane's company set an ambush at Two Bridges and was soon reinforced by Captain Jacob Ten Eyck's company from North Branch. When the loyalists arrived, there was a big fight. The loyalists "cut and ran" up North Branch River Road to Milltown, where they were able to ford the river by Cornelius Van Derveer's mill. (Milltown was at the end of Mill Lane just north of where Route 202 crosses the Raritan River.)

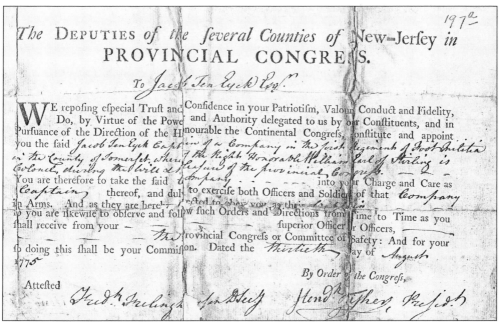

Jacob Ten Eyck from North Branch was given a commission as a Captain of Militia by the Provincial Congress of New Jersey. This is a copy of his commission. (Rutgers Special Collection.)

A list of all the Persons Names who are, to bring in wheate for the Army for the year 1779

	Bushels	
William Lane	40	to be Brought to Simons mills
John Ven Nest	6	to be Brought to do
Henry D Vroom	9	to be Brought do
Abraham Ten Eyk	12	to be Brought to Bankes
Widdow Bogert		to be Brought to Simons
Peter Dumont	20 of Inden	to do
John Bogart of weat 20 & 10 of Inden		to do
John Ettinger 10 Ry & 25 of Inden		to huff
Fradrick Atonson	4 of Inden	to do
Joseph Stevens 8 wheat		to do
George Hall 10 of Ry 10 of Inden		to do
Edword Hall 50 of Corn		to huff
John Huff 5 of do		to do
Lowrance Dumot 10 of wt & 10 of Ry		to do
George Hall 30 of Corn		to Simons
Wm Hall 24 of Corn		to do
Jacob Wickhoff 20 of Corn		to do
Andrus Ten Eyk 10 of wt		to Banker
Jerret Serbases 60 of Inden		to do
John Lane 20 of do		to do
James Duychinck 20 of do		to do
Thomas Thing 40 of do		to Berie
Robert Rosbrugh 10 wt		to Angles Mill
Mathew Lane 25 of Inden		to do
Mathias Lane Jur 20 of do		to do
Marion Hogemen 40 of do		to do
John Falkiner 20 wt		to do

A list of farmers in and around North Branch who supplied wheat and Indian corn for Washington's army in 1779. (Rutgers Special Collection.)

Many Branchburg farmers fought for American independence. John Smith is buried in the Vosseller burial ground. Just outside the fence of that small cemetery lie the bodies of ten Continental Army soldiers who fell ill and died while encamped at Two Bridges to guard the crossing one winter. (Branchburg Historic Preservation Commission.)

The Abraham Ten Eyck House sits up on the hill overlooking the confluence by Old York Road at Two Bridges. Abraham, a cousin of Captain Jacob Ten Eyck of North Branch, was Colonel of Militia for Somerset and Hunterdon Counties. On December 8, 1776, there was a skirmish in front of his house when about two hundred mounted loyalists attempted to cross the river to join the British in New Brunswick. A detachment of Continental troops camped below his house one winter. (Branchburg Historical Society.)

To Capt Jacob Ten Eyck.

224 1776 May 21

You are Desiresed to Distribute of the Powder in your Custity in the following manner — to Capt Stall at his Request 8 lb weight of Said Powder and also to Capt Roelof Sebring 5 Pounds and to the Bound Brook Company when their Captain Shall be Established 8 Pan and Preserve to your Self 7 Pounds weight and Take their Receipt for the Same —

May 21 1776 } By order of the Committee
Edward Bunn Chairman

Jacob Ten Eyck of North Branch was assigned to stockpile and guard gunpowder for the militia. This document orders him to issue varying amounts of gun powder to different militia captains. (Rutgers Special Collection.)

Hendrick Field carried this flintlock pistol and powder horn with him throughout the Revolutionary War. The pistol is one of very few of the kind made in London, England. Originally from Fieldville in Piscataway, Hendrick married Hannah Lane from North Branch and bought what is now the Lana Lobell farm on both sides of Lamington (Rattlesnake Bridge) Road in Bedminster for $5,000. (Ed Field.)

28

A Return of my District in Captain Ten Eik Compeny

	Guns	Bayonets	Cartuge Box	Rounds	Powder	Balls	Flints
George Auten Serjent	1		1	8	½	36	3
Philip V: arsdalen Corperel	1	1	1				
Cristiaun Faizer	1	1	1	8	½	6	2
2 James Ross							
Abraham V: sickelen							
Pawel Voorhais							
John Teepple			1	1	1		
George Teepple			1	1	1		
John V: arsdalen			1	1	1		
Abraham Britin			1	1	1		
Henry Beam			1	1	1		
Joseph Gaston							
Jacob Hoober							
william Chivis							
Roleph Huzzy							
John Powelson			1	1	1		
John Herried			1	1	1		
samuel smith			1	1	1		
	16		12 10	12 8	1 1	42	5

This list enumerates the equipment possessed by members of Captain Jacob Ten Eyck's militia company. (Rutgers Special Collection.)

During the Revolution, Guisbert Bogert owned this house. He also owned a slave named Samuel. Casper Berger from Readington Village asked Samuel to serve in the militia in his place. Samuel agreed and so Casper bought Samuel from Guisbert Bogert. Samuel fought in the Battle of Long Island, the skirmish at Two Bridges, and against British raiders in Hillsborough. He fought the Indians under General Sullivan all the way to Buffalo, New York. (Branchburg Historical Society.)

During the Revolution, this was Casper Berger's Tavern, a hotbed of patriot activity, and the meeting place for Captain David Schomp and his band of spies for General Washington. Samuel worked in the tavern, plowed the fields, and served his owner's military duty. After the war he requested his freedom, but it was denied. He was sold as a slave twice more before being permitted to work and purchase his own freedom. (Branchburg Historical Society.)

Three
The Young Republic

Victory in the American Revolution gave confidence to a young republic. Old York Road was white with covered wagons heading west with veterans who had been granted bounty land in the Northwest Territory. Architectural tastes turned to Federal and then Greek Revival styles alluding to our heritage of democracy from ancient Greece. George Vroom left home to seek his fortune at sea. The epitaph on his gravestone reads: "Tho Boreas blasts, and Neptun's waves, Have Cast me to & fro, In spite of all, By God's Decree, I'm anchored here below, While I at anchor, Here do ride, with many of our fleet, Yet once again, Shall I set sail, Our Admiral Christ to meet." (Branchburg Historic Preservation Commission.)

In 1790 Andrew Ten Eyck, son of Colonel Abraham Ten Eyck, married Sarah Berger, the daughter of Casper Berger of Readington. Abraham gave his son the back half of his farm, which ran from about where this house stands to the Hunterdon county line. Casper Berger, who was a mason, may have built the brick house. The front part and first-floor middle section were built in 1790 in the Federal style. The upper middle section was added later and the wood frame section in 1914. (Branchburg Historical Society.)

John Hardenberg operated a fulling (woolen) mill at Milltown in 1792. The property was later sold to Cornelius VanDerveer and passed down in his family. At one time there was a hamlet of seven dwellings, a gristmill, a sawmill, a fulling mill, a general store, a blacksmith shop, a grocery, a wheelwright, and a one-room schoolhouse, all on little Mill Lane, and all owned by the VanDerveer family. These are the ruins of one of the mills. (Branchburg Historical Society.)

This beautiful Federal-style brick home was the dwelling place of Cornelius VanDerveer, who owned the mills and the rest of Milltown. (Branchburg Historical Society.)

Another view of the Cornelius VanDerveer House showing a separate dwelling behind it. (Branchburg Historical Society.)

Four Pillars Farm. This Greek Revival-style mansion overlooking Pleasant Run was constructed by Peter T. Beekman in 1837. He owned and operated the Neshanic Mills. The farm was purchased in 1855 by Calvin Corle, who served as senator of New Jersey in the 1870s. He became president of the Somerset County Bank of Somerville from 1879 to 1893. The right wing was added to the mansion in the 1880s. During the 1940s the Bertram Goldsmiths lived here and operated the Pilfour Dairy. (Branchburg Historical Society.)

The DuMont House at the corner of Readington Road and Tanglewood Drive, built about 1835, is an example of a vernacular country Greek Revival house. (Branchburg Historical Society.)

Four
Churches

When the first settlers arrived, they brought the good book. For almost forty years there were no churches within an easy ride. This early Dutch Bible belonged to Joris Raplae, one of Bill Schleicher's ancestors, who came over in the 1600s. (Gardner A. Sage Memorial Library of the New Brunswick Theological Seminary.)

The Reverend Theodore Jacob Frelinghuysen leaves Holland for America. Frelinghuysen was Branchburg's first minister and began preaching on February 21, 1720, in the little log church. Among Christian scholars he is considered one of the greatest theologians of the colonial period, and is credited with paving the way for the Great Awakening. He had five sons who became ministers and three daughters who married ministers. His son John became our second minister. (*Christian History* Magazine.)

In 1717 a log church was built on the northwest corner of Old York Road and North Branch River Road. It was called "de Kerke over de Noord Branch." Theodore Jacob Frelinghuysen was the first minister. The church also served as town hall and school. It burned in 1737 and was rebuilt at Readington. Peter Dumont built his house on the foundation of the church and it was there that Queens College was located in 1779–80 when the British were in New Brunswick. (Branchburg Historical Society.)

Reverend Peter Studdiford was the sixth minister of the Readington Dutch Reformed Church, serving from 1786 to 1826. It was during Reverend Studdiford's tenure that services began to be held in English. Peter Studdiford lived in Branchburg on what is now the Kanach family's "River Lea Farm." Reverend Studdiford donated the land for Studdiford Drive so that school children from South Branch could get to the school without going all the way up to Two Bridges and back. (Walter Studdiford.)

The first church built at Readington was used from 1738 to 1833. Slaves attended church with their owners sitting in the balcony. It was not until after the American Revolution that services began to be conducted in English. Prior to 1800 Dutch was the primary language in this area and English was a secondary language. There was another church on this site from 1833 until the present structure was built in 1864. (Branchburg Historical Society.)

The fourth and present church in Readington was dedicated in 1865. The original steeple blew off in 1913. Casper Berger and his wife, along with Andrew Ten Eyck and his wife Sarah (Berger) Ten Eyck, are buried in the front yard. (Branchburg Historical Society.)

During the colonial period Dutch churchgoers brought their own Psalters (The Book of Psalms set to music). There were no hymns as we know them until 1796. This is the 23rd Psalm in Dutch set to music from *De Cl Psalmen des Propheten Davids*, printed in Amsterdam in 1749. (Gardner A. Sage Memorial Library of the New Brunswick Theological Seminary.)

The title page of an early Dutch Bible, such as were used by residents of Branchburg until the 1800s. (Gardner Sage Memorial Library of the New Brunswick Theological Seminary.)

The congregation of the Neshanic Dutch Reformed Church began to meet in 1752. The building took two years to build from Sourland Mountain stone beginning in 1759. It is the oldest church building in the county and beyond. The building cost 980 pounds, 11 shillings, and 5 pence to build. (Neshanic Station Historical Society.)

In 1825 a meeting was held in Abraham Dumont's barn of those people interested in establishing a church at North Branch. Over 1,000 people attended. The church was officially organized at the stone Ten Eyck House on September 10, 1825. This is the first building which was constructed of brick and completed about 1827. The last service held in this building was on October 4, 1863. The next day demolition began. (*The Address* . . . Reverend Philip Doolittle, 1906.)

A number of brick smoke houses in the village of North Branch were made from the bricks of the old North Branch church. (Branchburg Historical Society.)

The new church was dedicated in October 1864. Unfortunately, due to poor construction and reused materials, the building was declared to be unsafe for human occupancy within ten years. The building was completely reworked and rededicated March 9, 1875. This picture, showing the church looking very much as it does today, depicts the structure before the steeple blew off in a severe storm in February 1918. (Fred Heilich Collection, Branchburg Historical Society.)

The Reverend Philip Melanchthon Doolittle, D.D., served the North Branch church for fifty years. He was much loved by his congregation. In 1906 he wrote a short history of the church from which this picture was taken. (*The Address* . . . Reverend Doolittle, 1906.)

In February 1918 a severe storm blew the steeple off the North Branch Dutch Reformed Church. It was replaced by this belfry. A new steeple of the original type was reinstalled on the church in 1983 as a gift from George Greenaway in memory of his wife, Kathryn Dumont Greenaway. The belfry is now the gazebo at Kirkside, the house next door. (Fred Heilich Collection, Branchburg Historical Society.)

The North Branch Church Parsonage on Church Road behind the church. (Fred Heilich Collection, Branchburg Historical Society.)

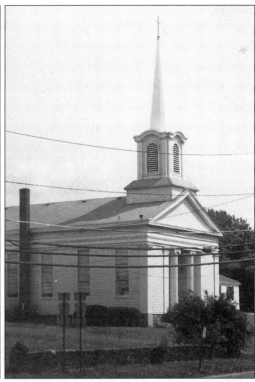

The Reformed Dutch Church of Branchville (South Branch) was erected in 1850 at a cost of $3,700. In 1854 President Chester Arthur occasionally worshiped here while visiting the Honorable F.T. Frelinghuysen at his summer home on the Raritan River. President Arthur made a gift of $25 to the church, and Senator Frelinghuysen presented the church with its first library. (Branchburg Historical Society.)

Reverend John Hendricks stoking the fire to warm the South Branch Reformed Church. (Somerset County Historical Society.)

In 1906, Judge John G. Schenck and other Methodists in Neshanic Station, weary of the 3-mile buggy ride to the church at Centerville, decided to build a church in the village. The lot was purchased for $350. It fell to John May, the first minister, to raise the money to build the church. He approached millionaire James B. Duke, who had made a fortune by building the American Tobacco Company. Reverend May told Mr. Duke that he needed $7,000 and asked him for $3,500. Duke said, "That's a lot of money, but if you can raise that much, I'll match it." Reverend May traveled to Philadelphia and obtained $500 from the Methodist denomination. While there he attended a bible study led by millionaire John Wanamaker, who was a Baptist. May told Wanamaker about Duke's offer, and Wanamaker quickly contributed enough money to make Duke pay up. The church cost about $6,800 to build and was dedicated in 1908. (Neshanic Station Historical Society.)

Five

Burnt Mills

In 1726 George Willocks, an East Jersey proprietor, sold this site to Daniel Axtell, son of the regicide of the same name. His father had been the Commander of the Guard in Westminster Hall during the trial of King Charles I. The King was convicted and beheaded. Many years later, when the King's son, Charles II, was restored to the throne, Axtell and the other regicides were themselves condemned to death. Axtel's son Daniel fled to the colonies where he became a wealthy merchant. Daniel's son William built the first mill at Burnt Mills. In 1754, he advertised in the *New York Gazette*: "A Compleat Mill, the house 60 by 40 feet with two Pairs of Stones, and a Room for a Third, or Convenience for a Fulling Mill under the same Roof, either of which will be erected at the Expense of the Owner, situate in the County of Somerset . . . near the North Branch of the Rariton River, on a large Stream . . ."

The mill was rented and later purchased by Andrew Leake, who named the location Bromley and also operated a general store there. His mill was to supply flour to Washington's army camped at Pluckemin following the Battle of Princeton in January 1777. Later that year, when he heard that a British foraging party was headed his way, Leake dumped all his flour and grain in the river to prevent them from capturing it. In reprisal, the British burned the mill and gave the village a new name. In 1779, while Washington was headquartered at the Wallace House, a home here served as the quarters for the Clothier General of the Continental Army.

The mill was rebuilt after the Civil War. This photograph was taken between 1903 and 1909. Mr. Erdley, the miller, and his wife Anna are standing in the doorway. Their daughter Mable is by the tree. A sideshot mill, it stood on the south side of the Lamington River just west of its junction with the North Branch. The old road passed in front of the mill, and the new bridge would have passed to the left of the photograph. The mill was torn down in 1928 by Kenneth B. Schley. (Clarence Dillon Library.)

This is the eighteenth-century house of the miller at Burnt Mills. (Branchburg Historic Preservation Commission.)

This abandoned old bridge crossing the North Branch of the Raritan River was once the main route from Branchburg to Bedminster. The current bridge was built across the Lamington River in 1927. (Branchburg Historic Preservation Commission.)

"Strawberry Fields." This beautiful vernacular Greek Revival house dates from the first half of the nineteenth century. The rear ell may be older. (Branchburg Historic Preservation Commission.)

The Gaston House on Burnt Mills Road (Bedminster), *c*. 1920. (Norma Finn Collection, Clarence Dillon Library.)

This is the schoolhouse at Burnt Mills as it looks today. It was brought from Pluckemin on rollers pulled by horses. It was first located next to the river, but later moved to its present site due to flooding. Today it is a private residence. Across the street, closer to the river, the old creamery is now also a private residence. (Branchburg Historical Society.)

Six
North Branch

A view of North Branch looking east with the F.C. Williams store on the left and the A.V. Vanderveer General Store and Post Office on the right. (Fred Heilich Collection, Branchburg Historical Society.)

This house is the oldest house in the village of North Branch. When it was built in the mid-1700s people lived in one part of the house and the farm animals lived in the other. (Branchburg Historic Preservation Commission.)

This is where the prosperous miller of North Branch lived. (Branchburg Historic Preservation Commission.)

The mill at North Branch. The mill was dismantled during World War II. (Fred Heilich Collection, Branchburg Historical Society.)

The mill race looking south from the bridge. (Fred Heilich Collection, Branchburg Historical Society.)

A view of North Branch looking east with the schoolhouse on the left. (Fred Heilich Collection, Branchburg Historical Society.)

The F.C. Williams store in North Branch Village (the current general store). Note the kerosene street lamp in front of the store. (Fred Heilich Collection, Branchburg Historical Society.)

The A.V. Vanderveer General Store and Post Office in North Branch, *c.* 1905. This is now a private residence across the street from the existing general store. (Fred Heilich Collection, Branchburg Historical Society.)

The A.V. Vanderveer General Store and Post Office in North Branch, *c.* 1918. (Neshanic Station Historical Society.)

The Low House at the southwest corner of Station Road and Route 28 in North Branch. This house was torn down in 1982. (Fred Heilich Collection, Branchburg Historical Society.)

A view of Depot Road, now Station Road, looking north toward the village of North Branch at the turn of the century. The house on the left was the Low House. (Fred Heilich Collection, Branchburg Historical Society.)

The original J.C. Glaser residence in North Branch. (Fred Heilich Collection, Branchburg Historical Society.)

The Henry Van Nest residence in North Branch Village, with Eleanor Jones Van Nest in the foreground. (Fred Heilich Collection, Branchburg Historical Society.)

The Flynn Smithy located on the north side of Old Turnpike Road west of Station Road. (Fred Heilich Collection, Branchburg Historical Society.)

The Wheelwright Shop at the corner of Old Turnpike Road (Route 28) and Burnt Mills Road in North Branch is now a private residence. Bill Wood is shown in front of the building. (Fred Heilich Collection, Branchburg Historical Society.)

The Riverview Inn at North Branch. (Fred Heilich Collection, The Branchburg Historical Society.)

Another view of the Riverview Inn in North Branch, now the North Branch Inn. (Neshanic Station Historical Society.)

A c. 1924 photograph of the iron truss bridge at North Branch that preceded the concrete bridge of today. (Neshanic Station Historical Society.)

The current concrete bridge was built on Route 28 in North Branch in 1924 to replace the iron truss bridge. (Lee Hamilton.)

A view of North Branch looking east showing the old iron truss bridge, with the North Branch Reformed Church in the background. (Fred Heilich Collection, Branchburg Historical Society.)

The iron truss bridge at North Branch, viewed across the mill pond from the north with the mill race going off to the right. This bridge was replaced with the present concrete structure in 1924. (Fred Heilich Collection, Branchburg Historical Society.)

The Bide-A-Wee Boarding and Rooming House on Burnt Mills Road. (Fred Heilich Collection, Branchburg Historical Society.)

The house on the south side of Old Turnpike Road (Route 28) to the left of the old post office. (Neshanic Historical Society.)

This house on the corner of Church Street and Route 28, originally a Ten Eyck house, is now the River Edge Antique Shop (Bridgewater). (Fred Heilich Collection, Branchburg Historical Society.)

The house at the corner of Church Street and Meadow Road in Bridgewater. (Fred Heilich Collection, Branchburg Historical Society.)

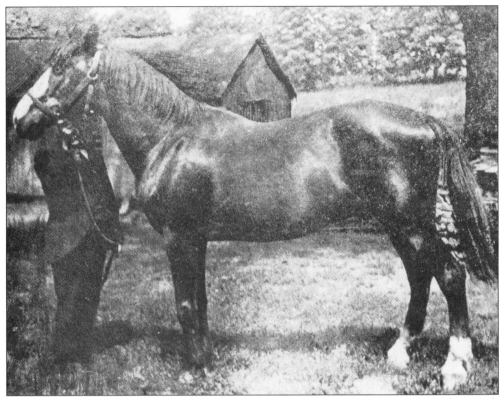

A thirty-four-year-old horse named "Billy" was the parsonage pet of the pastor of the North Branch Church. (Neshanic Station Historical Society.)

The North Branch Reformed Church Parsonage. (Neshanic Station Historical Society.)

The North Branch Reformed Church was split off from the Readington Church in 1825. This is the second church building, which was built in 1864. (Neshanic Station Historical Society.)

The Breezedale Farm on Burnt Mills Road. This house was destroyed by fire. (Fred Heilich Collection, Branchburg Historical Society.)

The Ralph Van Pelt residence on Burnt Mills Road looking north. (Fred Heilich Collection, Branchburg Historical Society.)

The Vesely Esso Service Center on Route 22 near North Branch in the late 1930s. This station is now the Albert Sons Amoco Station. (Neshanic Station Historical Society.)

Seven
North Branch Depot

The station master standing in front of the Central Railroad of New Jersey Station at North Branch Depot. This station burned down in 1971. (Neshanic Station Historical Society.)

The J.E. Glaser General Store at North Branch Depot. (Lee Hamilton.)

The J.E. Glaser residence at North Branch Depot. Mr. Glaser operated the general store at North Branch Depot and commissioned many of the postcards from which these pictures come. (Lee Hamilton.)

The creamery owned by George Field about 1918, with farmer's "tin lizzies" lined up outside to deliver milk by the can. The creamery burned in 1928, but the building was rebuilt. (Field family.)

George Field's house on the corner in the North Branch Depot (the same house as the J.E. Glaser residence, opposite). Richard Field is on the right, with a Trimmer boy on the left. (Field family.)

The North Branch Depot of the Central Railroad of New Jersey. (Fred Heilich Collection, Branchburg Historical Society.)

A view of Depot Road, now Station Road, looking south from near where Route 22 is today. (Fred Heilich Collection, Branchburg Historical Society.)

The station at North Branch Depot showing the stone arch bridge over the Chamber's Brook. This photograph was taken in 1969. (Branchburg Historic Preservation Commission.)

A view of the Central Railroad of New Jersey Depot at North Branch showing trackage and the J.E. Glaser General Store on the end of the creamery. (Fred Heilich Collection, Branchburg Historical Society.)

Eight
South Branch Village

Main Street, South Branch, at the turn of the century, looking west with the church on the left. The sender of this postcard wrote "There IS only one street!" Some things are better left unchanged. (Branchburg Historical Society.)

The Reformed Dutch Church of Branchville (see p. 43) was erected in 1850, according to the corner stone. The church was founded on May 14, 1850, and the building was dedicated January 27, 1851. The people of the village wanted a church, and a building fund was started as early as 1830. In 1842, a meeting was held in the schoolhouse (now the Little Red Schoolhouse in Branchburg) to get things going. The Amerman family donated the land for the church and cemetery, and the church cost $3,700 to build. Senator Frelinghuysen gave the Sunday school its first library, and subsequently donated additional volumes. (Neshanic Station Historical Society.)

This was the original parsonage for the South Branch Reformed Church. The house, which was completed in 1854, is now a private residence. (From the 125th Anniversary Booklet of the South Branch Church.)

The present parsonage was once the home of Peter Case, the village blacksmith, and his family. Mr. Case, his wife, and their daughter Anna sang in the choir. At about the age of fourteen she sang on Sunday nights for the guests of millionaire Diamond Jim Brady, who lived nearby. Anna Case later became a famous Soprano with the Metropolitan Opera in New York. In 1973 she donated this house to the church in memory of her parents. (From the 125th Anniversary Booklet of the South Branch Church.)

Pine Terrace, South Branch. (Neshanic Station Historical Society.)

The blacksmith shop in South Branch. Peter Case, father of famous Metropolitan Opera Star Anna Case, was the village blacksmith at the turn of the century. (Branchburg Historical Society.)

This house, across the street from the church, was once the home of Governor Peter D. Vroom. It was built about 1792. He was elected governor in 1829. (Branchburg Historical Society.)

This Italianate home on South Branch Road (Branchburg side of the river) was built around 1859. (Branchburg Historical Society.)

The South Branch Covered Bridge. The Reverend Dr. William S. Cranmer wrote: "While there was yet no church in that growing community, the Sunday teams (of horses) would turn magnificently into the cavernous mouth of the bridge and rattle across on their way to Readington Church or Raritan, the people exchanging greetings as they passed. Later, when the South Branch Church was built, the same teams would rattle in from far and near, or on week-days, head for the Bowman general store or haul up at the nearby Amerman distillery. It was a busy bridge, the feature of the landscape for which the traveler looked, the echoing voice for which he patiently listened. And once within its sheltered interior, its sides festooned with occasional posters announcing last season's fair, or harvest home, he could pause to shake the snow from his greatcoat of fur and, with the sulphur match that the outside blast would not tolerate, light the comforting pipe. Others too would sometimes rest within its welcoming shelter—an outlying tramp overtaken by too much indulgence in the cup that both cheers and inebriates; an amorous couple no longer sedate, their encircling arms unseen save by the dusty beams of sunlight filtering through; night prowlers on no good intent; perhaps a ghost or two, their spooky antics giving many a thrill to those who were fortunate enough to see such fearsome apparitions. We think also of the small boys ever climbing about and underneath it. There the waters ran darkly, sometimes turgid, swollen, sometimes quietly and as if spent, but always dark, in the shadows, where the wily bass was lurking, and whence the wily urchin sometimes drew a "big one." Well the old bridge has gone the way of all its wooden comrades and predecessors, and with it vanishes romance. To repair it, the practical ones tell us, would have cost almost as much as one of these cob-webby steel and concrete structures that the Freeholders very wisely favor. It's one of those things that's got to be—like the passing of grandpop when he was growing too old for medicines to mend, and too spent to endure longer the racket of modern life."

The South Branch Covered Bridge was built by Yocum Quick using wood he had salvaged from the Millstone Reformed Church when he rebuilt it in 1828. When this bridge was taken down in the early part of this century, some of the wood was used for the beams, paneling, and mantle in the "Tavern Room" of the Bowman House at the corner of Dreahook and Old York Road in Branchburg. This view is from the Branchburg side. (Neshanic Station Historical Society.)

The South Branch Covered Bridge was one of only two such bridges left in New Jersey when it was taken down. This view is from the South Branch side. Note the horse emerging from the bridge. (Neshanic Station Historical Society.)

The Van Doven (Doren) Cottage in South Branch. (Neshanic Station Historical Society.)

A river view of South Branch looking west from the bridge. (Neshanic Station Historical Society.)

Nine
Neshanic Station

Shadow Lawn, the largest and most beautiful home in Neshanic Station, was built by Judge John G. Schenck in 1858. At that time the area of the village was his farm. He landscaped his yard with exotic trees from all over the world, many of which survive today. Judge Schenck was a Republican state assemblyman in the 1860s and 1870s, and later a state senator. He was a director of the First National Bank of Somerville, which later became the Somerset Trust Company. He was also the state railroad commissioner, and a director of the South Branch Railroad Company.

During the 1870s and '80s, there was a series of financial collapses. When the area's fruit evaporating company failed in 1875, John Schenck was forced to sell off part of his land. In what was one of Somerset County's first sub-divisions, he laid out the village of Neshanic Station and sold house lots. When his tenant farmers and neighbors fell on hard times, he loaned them money and later forgave their debts. As a consequence of his generosity, he was finally forced into bankruptcy, and Shadow Lawn was sold at auction. In 1970, Shadow Lawn was used in the filming of the movie *The Witch's Sister*. (Neshanic Station Historical Society.)

A view of Maple Street from the west about 1920. (Neshanic Station Historical Society.)

A view of Elm Street, looking toward the river, *c.* 1920. (Neshanic Station Historical Society.)

Herter Quick on the back of his favorite horse about 1920. The horse is harnessed for farm work rather than riding. (Neshanic Station Historical Society.)

Herter Quick's residence on Maple Avenue in Neshanic Station in 1930. (Neshanic Station Historical Society.)

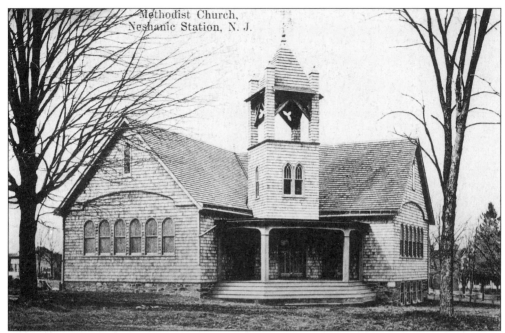

The Neshanic Station Methodist Church in 1908. John May, the first minister, raised money to build the church by appealing to rival millionaires James B. Duke and John Wanamaker (see p. 44). The church cost about $6,800 to build. (Neshanic Station Historical Society.)

The Fairview School in 1910. This school was replaced by the new brick Fairview School in 1914. (Neshanic Station Historical Society.)

The five-story Amerman Mill at the turn of the century. Today this is a private residence and part of the Neshanic Mills Historic District (Hillsborough). (Neshanic Station Historical Society.)

The Amerman Mill at Neshanic Mills showing the dam and mill pond. This c. 1908 photograph was taken from the Central Railroad bridge. (Branchburg Historical Society.)

The Central Railroad Station in 1906. All the buildings to the right of the station burned to the ground in the great fire of 1910. The Amerman Lumber Yard (now Jaeger) and the Holcomb Hotel are in the center of the photograph. (Neshanic Station Historical Society.)

The smoldering remains of the Neshanic Station business district after the great fire of 1910. The fire broke out in the creamery by the river. To fight the fire, a telegram was sent to the fire department in Somerville. There, a horse-drawn steam pumper was loaded on a railroad flat car and brought to Neshanic Station. In the mean time, the fire burned every building between the river and the railroad station. That the entire village did not burn is more attributable to a shift in the wind than to the arrival of the steam pumper. (Neshanic Station Historical Society.)

Somerville's Engine Company #1 about 1908 with the steam pumper that fought the great fire of 1910 in Neshanic Station. This pumper may still be seen at the Fireman's Museum in Somerville. (Charles F. Karbowski, Somerville Fireman's Museum.)

The Neshanic Volunteer Fire Company was formed after the 1910 fire. In 1943 the volunteers pose along side their 1929 Pirsch Pumper, in front of the old station house. They are, from left to right: (front) John Agans, Charles Lamken, and Pete Emery; (back) Irv Connet, John Caddis, John O'Brien, W.S. Dietz, A.B. Danberry, L.B. Lane, and Bob Sager. (G. William Amerman.)

The Neshanic Station Post Office. This one was replaced with the one now in use, and has become a private dwelling. (Neshanic Station Historical Society.)

The Lane Post Office and General Store in Neshanic (Hillsborough). (Neshanic Station Historical Society.)

The J. Bradford Opie General Store and Post Office is on the left. In the middle is the Rynearson harness shop, and on the right is the meeting hall of the Knights of Pythias—Junior Mechanic's League. (Neshanic Station Historical Society.)

The Holcomb Hotel was built in 1875 and destroyed in the fire of 1910. This picture is of the new hotel as rebuilt in 1910 and renamed the Neshanic Inn. (Neshanic Station Historical Society.)

Neshanic Vigilant Society.

FOR THE DETECTION
—OF—
HORSE THEIVES ETC.

OFFICERS:

A. A. CORTELYOU, President.   NELSON B. ROWLAND, 2nd. Vice President.
JNO. L. SCHENCK, 1st. Vice President.   M. MOUNT CORLE, Secretary & Treasurer.

DIRECTORS:

GEO. S. CORLE,   PETER T. HUFF
SAMUEL D. OPIE,   GARRET Q. BAIRD,
JAS. L. HALL,   ALEX. B. BROKAW.

PURSUERS:

WM. D. WYCKOFF,   JOS. C. S. LABAW,
L. J. HOAGLAND,   BEN. R. HOLCOMBE,
M. MOUNT CORLE,   PETER B. HALL,
CLYDE VAN NESTE,   F. J. STRINGER.

LIST OF MEMBERS:

Wm. L. Amerman,	B. J. Everette,	Henry V. Latourette,	Thos. A. Stryker,
Garret Q. Baird,	Peter B. Hall,	Cor. W. Miller,	Austin Thurston,
A. B. Brokaw,	H. R. Holcombe,	S. D. Opie,	D. J. Van Liew,
DeWitt Bowman,	L. J. Hoagland,	J. B. Opie,	Jno. T. Van Camp,
George Brokaw,	Peter T. Huff,	Jacob D. Quick,	A. G. Van Neste,
A. A. Cortelyou,	Rev. Jno. Hart,	N. B. Rowland,	P. P. Van Pelt,
D. B. Conover,	E. B. Hoagland,	Wm. L. Rowland,	Geo. Van Doren,
M. Mount Corle,	Peter R. Hall,	Isaac Stryker,	S. S. Van Fleet,
Theo. H. Case,	James L. Hall,	Wm. Shoemaker,	Peter Van Camp,
Jno. L. Corle,	R. W. Hoagland,	H. P. Sutton,	Clyde Van Neste,
Geo. S. Corle,	Peter A. Hoagland,	F. J. Stringer,	J. H. Van Dyke,
Calvin Corle,	A. W. Hall,	Jno. L. Schenck,	F. V. L. Wyckoff,
Jacob V. Case,	Sam'l C. Huff,	Jno. Stryker,	Wm. D. Wyckoff,
Chas. J. Corle,	I. H. Hill,	H. C. S. Schring,	J. W. Young,
Wm. H. Conover,	Jno. W. Kuhl,	Jno. S. Stryker,	H. W. Yorks,
Frank Cole,	J. C. S. Labaw	R. R. Stryker,	J. W. Thatcher
Wm. H. V. Davis,	Jno. C. Lane,		

C. E. Connet, Printer, Three Bridges, N. J.

The Neshanic Station Vigilant Society in 1920. The purpose of the society was to protect livestock. Members paid dues for protection. Pursuers were required to hunt for a certain period of time for stolen horses or other losses. If the loss was not recovered it was paid for out of the dues or assessments on members. Eventually they went broke. (Neshanic Station Historical Society.)

A view along Amwell Road in Neshanic (Hillsborough) about 1930. (Neshanic Station Historical Society.)

The original J.S. Covert & Sons building in 1923. This building burned down and was rebuilt as shown below. (G. William Amerman.)

The rebuilt J.S. Covert & Sons garage and store as it appeared in 1942. Covert was the biggest John Deere dealer in New Jersey from 1928 to 1987. They also sold Studebaker automobiles from 1937 to 1965. (G. William Amerman.)

The Metz Garage, c. 1914. Today this building houses the Neshanic Station barber shop. (Neshanic Station Historical Society.)

Earl and Ellis Dilts were the linemen who first brought electricity to the village in the 1926. Neshanic Station is on the end of the power line coming down the river from Glen Gardner and was always the one to suffer the longest outages. (Neshanic Station Historical Society.)

The Lehigh Railroad Station on Maple Street in Neshanic Station, with the creamery on the right, *c.* 1900. (Neshanic Station Historical Society.)

The New Jersey Central Railroad Station. The waiting room and ticket office were on the ground floor while the station master lived upstairs. This station still exists and has been restored by John Higgins to become a private residence. (Neshanic Station Historical Society.)

The old mill and the mill dam can be seen behind the New Jersey Central Railroad bridge at Neshanic Station in this 1930 photograph. This is a favorite fishing and swimming hole for area boys. (Neshanic Station Historical Society.)

The Elm Street Bridge connects Neshanic Station with Neshanic Mills in Hillsborough. Ordered from the catalogue of the Berlin (Connecticut) Bridge Company, it was erected in 1896. Of 1,000 such bridges ever constructed, only 50 still remain in the United States, and there is only one other in the state of New Jersey. It is listed on the National Register of Historic Places as part of Hillsborough's Neshanic Mills Historic District. This picture was taken about 1920. (Neshanic Station Historical Society.)

Peach trains of over one hundred cars would transport local fruit to the city markets, before a blight of San Jose scale killed all the trees. This picture shows such a train crossing the Lehigh Railroad trestle at Neshanic Station. (Neshanic Station Historical Society.)

River Scene. Neshanic Station, N. J.

The banks of the South Branch of the Raritan River near Neshanic Station have long been a good place to spend a summer afternoon. In years gone by, city folk spent their vacations at Shadow Lawn and other homes in the area and enjoyed the peaceful country life. This picture was taken about 1930. (Neshanic Station Historical Society.)

Ten
Centerville

The Swift Sure Stage Line. From colonial times, stage coaches carried passengers between New York and Philadelphia along Old York Road. Stopovers were made at Two Bridges, the White Oak Tavern, and Centerville. The coaches were green and red with gold trim and brass fittings. Coachmen wore buckskin breeches, high boots, a red vest, and a silk hat with a gold band and the brim turned up at the sides. The coach guard blew his horn at intervals from a half mile distant as they approached a village. The White Oak Tavern stood on Old York Road just east of the corner of Stony Brook Road. An ancient oak tree, for which the tavern was named, stood in the field near the bend in Old York Road. When passengers from Philadelphia saw the White Oak, they knew that they would soon be stopping for the night. Stages continued to operate into the beginning of this century. (Branchburg Historic Preservation Commission.)

The Centerville Tavern and Inn. The original building dating from before the American Revolution burned down in 1864. This building dates from approximately that time. The following advertisement appeared in the *Hunterdon Gazette* on January 3, 1827: "New York, Philadelphia Mail Stage, via New Hope, Flemington, Somerville, Bound Brook, Plainfield, Elizabethtown. Passengers in this line will leave Philadelphia at 8 o'clock A.M. on Mondays, Wednesdays and Fridays. Lodge at Centerville and arrive in New York at two P.M. of the succeeding days. Likewise leaving New York at half past ten A.M. of the days named above, stop at Centerville and reach Philadelphia at 4 P.M. of Tuesdays, Thursdays and Saturdays. Fare through $3.50, way passengers in proportion. All baggage at the risk of the owner." (Branchburg Historic Preservation Commission.)

The stagecoach barn did not burn in the fire that consumed the Centerville Inn. The following advertisement appeared in the *Hunterdon Gazette* on December 27, 1826: "Public sale on Saturday the 3rd of Feb. next on premises, the well known Tavern Stand and Stage House at Centerville being equi-distant from New York and Philadelphia on the Old Swift Sure Road. The house is large and commodious with a barn, shed, stables, ice house, etc. The lot contains 30 acres of first rate land meadow, arable and woodland. The Stages from New York and Philadelphia lodging at this house makes it worthy the attention of any purchaser." (Branchburg Historic Preservation Commission.)

The Centerville Blacksmith Shop. (Branchburg Historic Preservation Commission.)

The Centerville Methodist Church. Nicholas Egbert of Pleasant Run started the Methodist movement in the area. Egbert was dismissed from the Readington Reformed Church on September 10, 1788, for "erroneous Beliefs." Worship was held in a schoolhouse until this church was built in 1869. (Branchburg Historic Preservation Commission.)

Eleven
Branchburg in the Civil War

The drum of Billy Vosseller, drummer boy of the Rappahannock. At the age of fifteen, Billy Vosseller from Two Bridges volunteered to serve in the Civil War. He became the drummer boy for Company E of the 30th New Jersey Volunteer Infantry Regiment which was formed in Somerville in September 1862. Company A was raised in North Branch under Captain Arthur S. Ten Eyck, who was to rise to the rank of colonel and regimental commander. Company F was raised in Neshanic. The regiment was attached to the Grand Army of the Potomac under General "Fighting" Joe Hooker. This is Billy Vosseller's drum, which may be seen in the museum of the Somerset County Historical Society.

On August 4, 1862, President Lincoln called for men to be drafted from the militia or otherwise enlisted for a term of nine months. New Jersey was given a quota of 10, 478 men to fill by September. In order to avoid having a draft, it was decided to seek volunteers up to September 1, and then to draft the remaining number from those townships that had not met their quota. This system worked well and on September 2 there were already 10,800 volunteers in camp ready to be mustered. It had not been necessary to draft a single man.

In those days, men from a certain community would serve together in the same military unit. Men from Branchburg enlisted in the 30th New Jersey Volunteer Infantry Regiment. Company A was formed at North Branch under Captain Arthur S. Ten Eyck, who would rise to the rank of Lieutenant Colonel. Branchburg men also enlisted in Company E (formed in Somerville) and Company F (raised in Neshanic). The regiment was commanded by Colonel Alexander E. Donaldson, editor of the *Somerset Messenger*, and previously Brigadier General of the Somerset County Brigade of the New Jersey Militia.

The 30th New Jersey was made part of the Grand Army of the Potomac and assigned to post, railroad, and provost marshall duty. In December they were stationed at Falmouth, Virginia, opposite and below Fredericksburg. There, from across the Rappahannock River, they were able to witness the great battle where General Ambrose Burnside attempted to dislodge General Robert E. Lee from the impregnable heights of Fredericksburg. Over 11,000 Union troops died that day, in mostly suicidal assaults on the Rebel positions. The Rebels were not taken.

Early in 1863, the b30th New Jersey was ordered to Belle Plains, Virginia, and General "Fighting" Joe Hooker was assigned command of the Army of the Potomac. Captain Ten Eyck was promoted to Major on March 12, and to Lieutenant Colonel on April 5. From then on he commanded the regiment through most of its subsequent movements as a part of the 3rd Brigade, 1st Division, and 1st Army.

The objective remained to get the Rebels out of Fredericksburg and thus to open the way to Richmond. General Hooker planned to keep Lee's attention in Fredericksburg while he sent another force around the town to attack the Confederate flank, but just as the plan was a near success, Hooker hesitated and pulled back to a defensive position at Chancellorsville. General Lee then boldly moved to attack Hooker. He sent Stonewall Jackson to Hooker's right while he struck in the front. This action nearly cut the Union troops in two but they managed to set up a defensive line. Hooker retreated. The Rebel victory cost the life of Jackson, who was accidentally shot by one of his own men, and between 10,000 and 15,000 soldiers on each side. A like number were wounded.

There were many skirmishes, but no decisive engagements as the Army of the Potomac moved to re-cross the Rappahannock River. It was the 30th New Jersey that was one of the last units to cross the river, covering the orderly withdrawal of the Union forces. Soon the term of service for the soldiers of the 30th expired, and they returned home. None had been killed in action, but a number had died of disease, a few in the very last days of their term of service.

At first the farmers of Branchburg didn't see much action, but were assigned to supply functions. One of their details called for transporting, deploying, and dismantling pontoon bridges as depicted here. (*Frank Leslie's Illustrated Newspaper*, January 3, 1863.)

The 30th New Jersey witnessed but did not participate in the Battle of Fredricksburg, Virginia. Shortly after, in May 1863, they were in the Battle of Chancellorsville. The Confederate army was led by General Robert E. Lee. Over 30,000 men were killed or wounded in two days of fighting, including General Hooker (who recovered) and General "Stonewall" Jackson (who was accidentally shot by one of his own men and died a few days later). (Branchburg Historical Society.)

THE DRUMMER OF THE RAPPAHAN-NOCK.

BY J. W. WATSON.

THE long roll!
Sharp with the breaking of the morn,
  Four score of thousands spring to life.
They who have dreamed upon their swords
  All night, about the coming strife.
Full eighty thousand eager men,
  With burning eyes and nervous hand,
Await on Rappahannock's shore
  The stern command,
      Forward!

The fifer shrill
Calls from each wooded spot and hill
  The busy hosts to line.
The sturdy tramping picket guard
  Exchange the countersign,
A thousand hurrying hands strike tents
  At bugle call,
And thrice ten thousand hearts beat time
  In echo to the rise and fall
Of the wild music rhyme,
  That fills and dances in the morning air.

Loud over all the rumbling train
  The pontoons bear,
While from the farther shore
  The cannon's blare
Heaves grape and cannister like rain
  About the engineers;
And riflemen, with deadly aim, look out
  From each redoubt.

"Up men, your comrades fall like sheep,
  Their corses strew the shore,
The rebels, from their hiding holes,
  Bathe loyal breasts in gore.
Up to your work, stout northern hearts,
  The cowards must be sped;
Mark every recreant, skulking wretch,
  And leave him with the dead.

"A hundred men to volunteer!
  A hundred men I seek!
A hundred men, your general calls!
  Who will be first to speak?"
And then, as with one mighty voice,
  A hundred score spake out,
And all the woods and valleys round
  Returned the glorious shout.

Deep laden with a hundred men
  Picked from the bold and brave,
The frail boats floated from the shore,
  On Rappahannock's wave.
But ere their gunwales kissed the stream
  A stout lad leaped aboard,
No musket filled his boyish hands,
  Nor held they eager sword.

He pointed to his well-worn drum,
  And begged they'd take him o'er,
"You'll want a drummer, captain, when
  You reach the other shore."
The captain looked half wondering,
  Half pitying, in his face,
"No boy, with us your life is gone,
  This is the safer place."

"The safer place! why I can die,
  So that my country gain!"
With downcast eyes he seeks the shore,
  His every plea in vain.
He aids to push the laden boats
  Through icy waves and wind,
But one bears more than stand within—
  The drummer clings behind.

      Whew!
How sing the noisy shell
Like messengers from hell,
      Around the fleet!
And how like summer rain,
Against the window pane,
      The balls patter down!
Through clouds of smoke and fire,
The boats are drawing nigher
      To the shore!
The rowers, almost blind,
Watch the drummer cling behind,
      With a smile.

The bank is reached at last,
But the drummer stands aghast,
  For a splinter of the blast,
      Strikes his drum,
      And 'tis dumb.
But a moment does he stand,
Then with musket in his hand
He joins the gallant band
      In the charge.
With a shot, a thrust and shout,
They spring to each redoubt,
And they clear the rebels out
      With a run.
But the drummer you will find
No longer clings behind,
He is fleeter than the wind
      On the front!

"Hail Columbia! happy land!"
  Thy spirit is not dead;
The drummer is but of the fire
  That burneth fierce and red.
The fire that warmed our father's blood,
  That flowed at Bunker Hill,
Within a score of million veins
  Is glowing fiercely still.

Our hands are nervous for the fight,
  The right must always win,
God sits in judgment on the hosts
  Amid the battle's din;
And when he suffers right to fall
  'Tis but to rise again.
Against the spirit of our land
  Rebellion strikes in vain.

The drummer boy of the Rappahannock. (*Frank Leslie's Illustrated Newspaper*, May 16, 1863.)

Twelve
The Railroads

The Elizabethtown and Somerville Railroad was chartered in 1831, and opened to Somerville in 1842. This is the kind of engine that ran on that railroad when it opened. In 1847 the Somerville and Easton Railroad was chartered to continue the line to Phillipsburg. The two railroads merged in 1849 to form the Central Railroad of New Jersey. (Branchburg Historical Society.)

North Branch Depot showing the station and the stone arch bridge over Chamber's Brook. Note the manned crossing control tower near the center of the photograph. Glaser's residence and general store are between the tower and the station. (Fred Heilich Collection, Branchburg Historical Society.)

The station at North Branch Depot as it appeared in 1960. It burned down in 1971. The upstairs of the station was the dwelling of the station master. (Branchburg Historic Preservation Commission.)

North Branch Depot looking west from the wooden bridge. A "peddler freight" is "in the hole" (on the siding), waiting for a more important train on the main line to pass. (Fred Heilich Collection, Branchburg Historical Society.)

The rail crossing at North Branch Depot showing the J.E. Glaser residence on the left, and his general store on the end of the creamery on the right. (Fred Heilich Collection, Branchburg Historical Society.)

The stone arch bridge of the Central Railroad of New Jersey at North Branch was built in 1847 on dry land on the Branchburg side of the river. When it was finished, the river was diverted to flow under it, causing Branchburg to lose some land to Bridgewater. (Fred Heilich Collection, Branchburg Historical Society.)

Engine #107 of the Central Railroad of New Jersey on a special excursion to Lake Hopatcong in the 1880s. (Somerset County Historical Society.)

Engine #1286 at Neshanic Station. (Somerset County Historical Society.)

The Lehigh Valley Railroad Station in Neshanic Station. (Neshanic Station Historical Society.)

"Camel-back" Engine #770 of the Central Railroad of New Jersey at Neshanic Station in 1952. (Neshanic Station Historical Society.)

A diesel locomotive on the Central Railroad line in 1956 shortly before it was closed down. (Bill Amerman.)

The main line of the Lehigh Valley Railroad going into Neshanic Station. The creamery is to the right of the tracks. Fairview Drive is on the left and Woodfern Road is on the right. (Neshanic Station Historical Society.)

Thirteen
Agriculture

Cows in the corn. Until the 1970s there were more cows than people in Branchburg. These cows are chewing their cud on the Staats farm, *c.* 1965. (Grace Staats.)

A *c.* 1953 photograph of the Ten Eyck, Vandervere farm (1725), showing the barn on the left that is no longer there. This is a "Bi-centennial" farm, which means it has been in the same family for over two hundred years. At this time, it still belongs to a descendant of the original builder. (Lee Hamilton.)

A farmer preparing his field the old fashioned way, with a horse and plow. (Grace Staats.)

This dairy farm owned by William Higgins and handed down to his son, J.J. Higgins, was at the corner of Readington Road and Route 22. The large white cow barn burned down about 1935. The house and other buildings were demolsihed in 1990. (Wilma Farley Blaufuss.)

Mowing hay on the Frank Lane farm about 1936. The Lane farm was on Readington Road between Station Road and the railroad tracks. (Wilma Farley Blaufuss.)

The Housel farm on South Branch Road is one of the oldest farms in the area dating back over 250 years. The farm has one of the last remaining operating windmill well pumps in the area. (Branchburg Historic Preservation Commission.)

Haying on the Eyck farm. The two men are holding pitch forks which they have used to pitch the hay up on the wagon. When they get back to the barn, they will use the forks to pitch the hay up in the loft. (Mrs. William Stryker.)

This farm on the south side of Old York Road west of Route 202 was owned by William P. Bowman. The Phillips family lived here and farmed the place. The picture was taken from the top of the electrical tower in 1930. Today the barns are gone and the house belongs to the Branchburg Historical Society. Note the other farm on the distant right which was where Roche Diagnostics is today. (Branchburg Historical Society.)

Plowing in 1920 with a Fordson tractor. (Branchburg Historical Society.)

Disking a field on the Lane farm on Readington Road in the 1920s. (Wilma Farley Blaufuss.)

An aerial view of the Pilfour Dairy taken by Bill Amerman in 1940. The dairy was run by Mr. and Mrs. Bertram Goldsmith on Four Pillars Farm at the corner of South Branch Road and Pleasant Run Road (see p. 34). (G.W. Amerman.)

Five-year-old Drew Housel at the turn of the century feeding chickens on what is now the Hunter farm. (George Hunter.)

Left: The Staats farm on Harlan School Road during the 1940s. Note the Dutch barn in the background. (Grace Staats.)
Right: A c. 1950 photograph of John Staats with his sons: Jim is at the wheel, with Bill on the right. (Grace Staats.)

A c. 1940 aerial view of the Staats farm on Harlan School Road. (Grace Staats.)

James J. Staats and his dog Shep, aging pork on the Staats farm, *c.* 1948. (Grace Staats.)

The Van Arsdale farm on Whiton Road, now the elementary school site. (Grace Staats.)

The interior of the old Dutch barn that now belongs to the county on South Branch Road. The huge, hand-hewn timber "H" frame and the entrance on the gable end are characteristic of a Dutch barn. Animals were kept in each side. Hay was stored on top of poles resting on the anchor beams. Wagons were kept underneath on the main floor that also served as a threshing floor. (Branchburg Historic Preservation Commission.)

Fourteen
The Old Schools

The one-room public school at North Branch, *c.* 1890. This school was built in 1886. (Fred Heilich Collection, Branchburg Historical Society.)

At a meeting of the Proprietors of the Schoolhouse held yesterday, the expence of erecting and finishing the said Schoolhouse was calculated, when it was found to amount to near thirty Pounds. ___

But the proprietors being generously disposed to make no account of the Timber, or a great part of their labour, if they can only collect as much money from those which has not assisted at the building, as will defray the expence of Boards, Nails, the making of the Shingles, &c. have agreed to the following Sums, to be paid in Wheat, or Money, within two Months after date, which if complied with on the part of the subscribers, it shall Intitle them to a right in the Schoolhouse, in as full, and Ample a manner, as if they had assisted at the building of it. ___

N. Branch 30, Oct. 1782.

Jacob Tenick ½ Bushel Wheat
Joseph Stull ½ Bushels of W

The first school in Branchburg was the log church at Two Bridges which began as a church and school in 1720. This is an agreement to build a school at North Branch in 1782. (Rutgers Special Collection.)

The North Branch Schoolhouse in 1906. (Neshanic Station Historical Society.)

The North Branch School after an additional classroom had been added. The school became a firehouse after the Old York School was built in 1950. (Branchburg Board of Education Publication.)

Pupils at the South Branch School (Little Red Schoolhouse) in 1910. From left to right are: (front row) Elizabeth Hipple, Alice Fisher, Irwin Van Cleef, David Thompson, DeWitt Bowman Jr. (whose father ran the general store and was the county treasurer), Lurell Case, Greer Van Nest, Fred Quick, Clifford Baird, and Abraham Stryker; (middle row) Mathilda Van Nest, Elizabeth Stryker, Andrew Housel, Bergen Dalley, Harold Butterfield, Milton Van Nest, Stanley and Lester Case (son of the local blacksmith and brothers of opera star Anna Case), and William Gillette; (back row) Anna May Strathey, Esther Van Nest, Nary Van Nest, Mary Stryker, Elizabeth Robotham (teacher), Marion Van Fleet (mother of actor Lee Van Cleef), Louise Quick, Florence Case, Meta Thompson, Viola Van Horn, and Emmaline Gillette. (Drew Housel.)

The South Branch School (Little Red Schoolhouse) was built in 1832. (Grace Staats.)

Fairview School in Neshanic Station around the turn of the century. (Neshanic Station Historical Society.)

The "new" Fairview School was built on Marshal Street in Neshanic Station in 1914 to replace the old school. Unfortunately, it was never considered safe to use the upstairs. This school was demolished after the Old York School was built in 1950. (Branchburg Board of Education Publication.)

The Milltown School about 1902. Built about 1845 behind the brick house at the end of Mill Lane, it had by this time been moved up the hill to the site of the Cedar Grove School, because the children were too noisy for the miller, Michael Vander Veer, and his wife. It had a pot belly stove in the middle of the room, and a wooden bench around three walls (school desks hadn't been invented yet). (Wilma Farley Blaufuss.)

Three pupils on the front porch of the Milltown School. Prior to this fine structure being built in 1842, school was taught in the upstairs of an old building with swine living downstairs. The upstairs was actually cantilevered over the mill race. This made it possible for schoolboys to fish through knotholes in the floor when the teacher wasn't looking. It has been recorded that at least one time class was disrupted by the catching of a fish. (Wilma Farley Blaufuss.)

126

The Harlan School, formerly located at the northeast corner of Harlan School Road and Readington Road. This school was used until the Old York School was built in 1950. It then became a private residence and was demolished by the developer of that site in 1992. (Neshanic Station Historical Society.)

The Cedar Grove School was built in 1923 to replace the school on the facing page. It had two school rooms and served until the Old York School was built in 1950. It then became the municipal building. (Branchburg Board of Education Publication.)

The Class of 1919 at the Burnt Mills School with Mrs. Abram Ten Eyck as teacher. The students are, from left to right: (front row) Margaret Osborne, Elmer Reger, Simon Nivius, Eddie Tiesher, William Cole, John Nevius, and Roy Vanderveer; (back row) Emma Walsh, Hazel Hatman, Dora Walsh, Elsie Teisher, William Milner, William Tiesher, Myrtle Hindershot, Edna Green, Margaret Nevins, and Gertrude Hindershot. (Carol Philhower.)

The Burnt Mills Schoolhouse was brought from Pluckemin on rollers pulled by horses. Mrs. Ten Eyck was paid $675 her first year, but by her third year she was the highest paid teacher in Bedminster at $1,300 per year. She taught at the school from 1918 to 1927. She first boarded with Frank Regan, who owned the grist mill on the Branchburg side of the river. Later she married his cousin, Abram Ten Eyck, who later operated the North Branch general store. (Carol Philhower.)

Fifteen
A Few Famous Folks

A c. 1905 photograph of the Bowman family. (Bowman family photograph, Eric Smith.)

"Diamond Jim" (James Buchanan) Brady (1856–1917). Diamond Jim Brady, having amassed a fortune as a railroad equipment salesman and investor, bought Ellesdale Manor Farm in 1901 for $86,000 from Mr. McCutcheon, president of the Consolidated Playing Card Company. Diamond Jim chose South Branch because it was half way between New York City and Philadelphia, the two cities where he transacted most of his business. Everything used in decorating the house and outfitting the farm had to be the best and most expensive, even down to the gold-plated buckets used for milking the cows when Jim felt the need to impress visiting railroad magnates. The livestock were the finest that money could buy. Manure was imported to ensure that the crops were of prize-winning quality. The farm produced so much foodstuff that even with all the dinner parties that Jim could throw, and the feeding of the staff, they could not consume it all. The chauffeur became too fat to sit behind the steering wheel, so Jim made him a night watchman. Jim didn't want to sell the excess food because it would take money away from the local farmers. So he decided to give it away to his friends, his employees, and the less fortunate in the theater community of New York City. Jim had huge insulated zinc hampers constructed which he would fill with butter, milk and cheese, squab, celery, eggs, beets, carrots, cauliflower, radishes, corn, asparagus, and loaves of fresh baked bread.

Anna Case, daughter of the local blacksmith, was about fourteen years old when she sang for Diamond Jim and his guests. Perhaps it was this that influenced her to seek a career in the theater. She began with the Metropolitan Opera in 1909 and became a famous soprano in the years before 1920. She later became a concert singer. She was a favorite of Thomas Edison and may be heard on about one hundred of his recordings. Anna became the mistress of multimillionaire Clarence Mackey, whose wife had previously left him. They were later married. Mackey's daughter Ellin eventually married famous song writer Irving Berlin. (Branchburg Historical Society.)

Left: "Jersey Lily" Lillie Langtry, the actress and singer who won the west, had previously won the heart of Diamond Jim Brady. (Branchburg Historical Society.)

Right: Lillian Russell, the famous actress and singer, was a frequent house guest at Diamond Jim Brady's estate in South Branch. (Branchburg Historical Society.)

"Ellesdale Manor Farm," the country estate of Diamond Jim Brady, lies just north of the village of South Branch on River Road. "Going down to the Brady's Farm" became a fashionable thing to do. Jim threw weekend parties that would sometimes last four days. Lillian Russell and Flo Ziegfield were frequent guests with many others from Broadway and Wall Street. Sometimes Miss Russell would stay through the week to rest up for the next party. Regular Sunday night dinner guests were entertained by a beautiful little village girl named Anna Case, who came to sing. (Branchburg Historical Society.)

Four Oaks Farm on Burnt Mills Road, the estate of Count and Countess Eccles. During the American Revolution this was a Beekman farm which they called Oak Hill farm. Over the years the original farmhouse was enlarged and expanded. The columns were added about 1920 by a Beekman descendant. In 1943 the property was purchased by Donald and Mary Hyde. He was a lawyer, and she later earned a Ph.D. Together they established an extensive collection of rare books, and added a wing to the house to house the collection. They renamed the estate Four Oaks Farm. Sometime after the death of Donald Hyde, his widow married Count Eccles, currently a member of the English House of Lords. (Branchburg Historical Society.)

"Riverside" on Lamington Road at the river. In 1903, Henry Orsenigo, an Italian immigrant, founded a furniture business in New York. In 1923 he bought a small house on this site and began its expansion to the current configuration. Italian craftsmen from his factory did most of the work, including pegged satinwood and teakwood floors, hand-carved decorations and cabinets, exposed ceiling beams, and closets with mahogany and rosewood interiors. (Branchburg Historical Society.)

Dakin House, the guest house and conference center for the Merck Pharmaceutical Corporation, located on River Road at the Merck farm, was originally a nineteenth-century farmhouse. It was purchased by a wealthy New York financier named Dakin who altered and expanded the structure into this fine country estate. (Branchburg Historical Society.)

Dakin House, c. 1912. Note the unusual wavy pattern to the art deco brick and stone wall in front of the house. (Branchburg Historical Society.)

An engraving of William P. Bowman commissioned by the Roebling Company. Mr. Bowman had made his fortune as manager of the New York office of the John A. Roebling Sons Company, the steel company which had constructed the Brooklyn Bridge and many other suspension bridges. His work took him on many trips to Europe and South Africa. William Bowman and his son each served as president of the Raritan Valley Country Club. (Bowman family photograph, Eric Smith.)

A view of the Bowman estate from Old York Road in the late 1920s. This estate, built in 1911 by William P. Bowman from South Branch, was named "White Oak Tavern," after the stage coach tavern which at that time still existed, neglected and forlorn on the nearby corner of Old York Road and Stony Brook Road. The estate consisted of almost 200 acres, extending all the way to Route 202. (Bowman family photograph, Eric Smith.)

A view of the Bowman estate, "White Oak Tavern," from Dreahook Road in the late 1920s. The Bowman mansion consisted of seventeen rooms, including servants quarters. Outbuildings included barns, an ice house, a garage, a cottage, an engine room, a tool house, a wood house, a work shed, and a root cellar. (Bowman family photograph, Eric Smith.)

The central entry hall to the Bowman House and the main staircase to the upstairs in the late 1920s. (Bowman family photograph, Eric Smith.)

Above: The living room of the Bowman House as it was furnished in the late 1920s. (Bowman family photograph, Eric Smith.)

A view of the Bowman House in 1926 showing the servant's porch, the double window to the servant's dining room, and the eyebrow window to the maid's bedroom. (Bowman family photograph, Eric Smith.)

Opposite: The "Tavern Room" was the favorite place to entertain close friends. The wall paneling, the ceiling beams, and the mantle came from the South Branch Covered Bridge when it was torn down in 1914. The old bridge had been built in 1835 by Yocum Quick from wood he had salvaged from the Millstone Reformed Church, which he had rebuilt in 1828. The previous church at Millstone from which this wood had been taken had survived several skirmishes and the burning of the courthouse at Millstone (then Somerset Courthouse). In the wood of Bowman's "Tavern Room" may still be seen musket ball holes from those Revolutionary War battles. The Bowmans entertained many famous guests in this room and invited them to carve their names in the top of the trestle table shown on the right side of the photograph. Among the names carved in the table are President Warren G. Harding, Senator Joseph S. Frelinghuysen, Ferdinand and Ruth Roebling, George Post, George Bogart, and Louis Paul Dessar. (Bowman family photograph, Eric Smith.)

A visit from Teddy Roosevelt in about 1912. The remains of this same lawn furniture, which also appears in many other Bowman family photographs over the years, may still be seen in the cellar of the house. (Bowman family photograph, Eric Smith.)

A companion to the previous picture. This time William P. Bowman has replaced the former president behind the table. (Bowman family photograph, Eric Smith.)

People gather for a golf tournament at the Bowman estate, *c.* 1920. (Bowman family photograph, Eric Smith.)

Branchburg's first golf course was at the corner of Old York Road across the street from the Bowman House, where this tournament was held about 1920. (Bowman family photograph, Eric Smith.)

President Warren G. Harding and Senator Frelinghuysen playing golf at the Raritan Valley Country Club in 1921. While playing, a messenger arrived with the Knox Porter Resolution for the President's signature—the measure that officially ended World War I. William P. Bowman, a charter member of the club and a member of the New Jersey Republican Committee, entertained President Harding at his home in Branchburg where the President carved his name in the "Tavern Room" table. (Bowman family photograph, Eric Smith.)

William P. Bowman and his daughter-in-law Dorothy in the garden of the estate, with the ice house in the background, on July 5, 1927. (Bowman family photograph, Eric Smith.)

Francis Bartow Bowman (son of William P. Bowman) and his bride Dorothy Giles Bowman. The Bowmans are on their honeymoon in Europe in 1926, and stand in front of the plane that took them across the English channel. Francis later became vice president of Chase Manhattan Bank in New York. (Bowman family photograph, Eric Smith.)

Baggage stickers from the Bowman's 1926 honeymoon trip to London and Paris. (William A. Schleicher IV.)

Practicing golf swings in front of the house in 1926. Dorothy Giles Bowman (right) was an avid golfer and started the woman's golf leagues at the Raritan Valley Country Club. (Bowman family photograph, Eric Smith.)

Playing croquet on the lawn. Dorothy Giles Bowman is in the middle, with her brother Arthur N. Giles on the left. (Bowman family photograph, Eric Smith.)

Playing softball on the lawn. Fred Meyers is sliding into base while Madeline Giles (Dorothy's mother) is catching. (Bowman family photograph, Eric Smith.)

Jean Jewett holding the horse's bridle with Dorothy Giles Bowman on the right about 1927. (Bowman family photograph, Eric Smith.)

The 1926 Packard 6 open touring car belonging to Francis and Dorothy Bowman when they were married. (Bowman family photograph, Eric Smith.)

In front of the Bowman House, Francis and Dorothy (on the right) stand with friends by their 1926 Packard 6. (Bowman family photograph, Eric Smith.)

Dorothy Giles Bowman at the wheel of
their 1926 Packard 6 in front of the
house in 1927. (Bowman family
photograph, Eric Smith.)

The garden path behind the Bowman
estate in 1927. (Bowman family
photograph, Eric Smith.)

A late 1940s aerial view of the Silver Saddle Ranch on Readington Road. In 1935, Biagio D'Angelo, a manufacturer of women's coats and suits in New York, bought the house at the southwest corner of Readington Road and D'Angelo Drive as a place for weekends and summer vacations. "In those days," his daughter Marie said, "you could walk down the middle of Readington Road all day long and never see a car." (Marie Harwitt.)

Biagio D'Angelo's daughter Marie married Norman Harwitt, who was a friend of Buster Crabbe, the famous actor who had played Tarzan, Buck Rodgers, and was in scores of westerns during the 1930s. Biagio D'Angelo and Buster Crabbe became partners in the operation of the Silver Saddle Ranch. They held rodeos, Wild West shows, hay rides, and water shows at the pool. The first time they held a show the traffic was backed up all the way to the Somerville Circle. The Italianate house next door to the pool on Harlan School Road was at that time a restaurant and boarding house. This is a copy of their business card. (Marie Harwitt.)

A local girl who lived across Readington Road from the Silver Saddle Ranch became a trick rider. Here she is seen putting Black Star through his paces at one of the shows. (Marie Harwitt.)

A clown act at the Silver Saddle Ranch in the late 1940s. (Marie Harwitt.)

Thor Solberg was an aviation pioneer. Born in Norway in 1893, he came to the United States in the 1920s and learned to fly at Roosevelt Field on Long Island, where Charles Lindberg began his famous flight. Thor dreamed of being the first to fly from New York to Norway. On July 16, 1935, he took off to realize his dream. (Solberg family photograph.)

The *Leiv Eiriksson*, the open cockpit amphibian biplane flown by Thor Solberg on his pioneer trip to Norway in the summer of 1935. It was not a non-stop flight, hopping instead from New York, to Montreal, Newfoundland, Greenland, Iceland, and the Faroe Islands before landing in the harbor of Bergen, Norway, on August 16. The route Thor Solberg pioneered is almost the same route used today by commercial air traffic. (Solberg family photograph.)

For his great achievement, Thor Solberg was decorated with Norway's highest civilian award, the St. Olaf Cross, by King Haakon VII. He was also presented with a medal from the King of Denmark. Hitler offered him the Iron Cross, but he refused it. (Solberg family photograph.)

In 1939, Thor Solberg bought a farm in Readington to establish the Solberg-Hunterdon Airport. This is an aerial view of Solberg Airport, which was surrounded by farm land when it was first opened in 1941. During World War II Solberg trained over 5,000 pilots for the Army Air Corps here and in Massachusetts, with a perfect safety record. (Solberg family photograph.)

Photo: Vang Stud

Two views of Solberg Airport at the time it was first opened in 1941. In 1939, Solberg advised President Roosevelt that, given the range of German bombers, they could bomb the U.S. from bases in Iceland and Greenland and return to the same bases. Acting on Solberg's advice, Roosevelt found that the Germans had already begun to implement such plans. Thereafter, American bases were established to protect our northern boarder. (Solberg family photograph.)

A view of Solberg Airport about 1949. (Solberg family photograph.)

The Solberg Aviation building was located on Route 22 in Branchburg just west of the current Summit Bank branch office. From this building he sold airplanes and automobiles. There was a runway over 1,000 feet long behind the building. The 1950 Cadillac belonged to Thor Solberg. Later, this became a bowling alley also owned and operated by the Solberg family. The building was demolished in the early 1980s. (Solberg family photograph.)

The Playhouse Theatre

Coming SATURDAY, FEB. 26th AT 8:00 P.M. ▼▼▼

In Person
Thor
SOLBERG
NOTED EXPLORER

Benefit of
VETERANS of FOREIGN WARS
DEPT. OF RHODE ISLAND

MOVIES OF
RETRACED ROUTE
of LEIV EIRIKSSON

Solberg's feat created a sensation. He was invited to appear and speak, and people flocked to see him. (Solberg family photograph.)

Thor Solberg in the cockpit of a stunt biplane. The wording on the side of the fuselage warns: "Important Remove Battery and Contents (of) Luggage Compartment Before Aerobatics." (Solberg family photograph.)

Solberg Field about 1949. (Solberg family photograph.)

Sixteen
Town Folk

At the 1965 Memorial Day Parade in Neshanic Station the Honorable Assemblyman Christopher (Kip) S. Bateman carries the flag of his cub scout den. Kip came to politics naturally following in the footsteps of his father, the Honorable Senator Raymond (Ray) Bateman. (Bateman family photograph.)

Left: In 1861, Justice of the Peace Sylvester Robins lived in the former Guisbert Bogert House on North Branch River Road (see p. 30). Robins Road was named after him. (Somerset County Historical Society.)

Right: Calvin Corle, state senator in the 1870s and president of the Somerset County Bank in Somerville, lived at Four Pillars Farm (see p. 34). (Snell, *History of Hunterdon and Somerset Counties*, 1881.)

Mr. and Mrs. Nevins, dressed in their Sunday best, set off for church. (Neshanic Station Historical Society.)

The ragman's wagon came around periodically to collect old clothing and rags. (Branchburg Historical Society.)

The Knights of Pythius, Young Mechanics League baseball team, *c.* 1920, in Neshanic Station. From left to right are: (front row) Doug Hoff and Lester Gulick; (back row) Russell "Boots" Edgar, Russell Cray, Wes Horner, Fred Allegar, George Amerman, Maurice Grescom, and Daniel Amerman. (G. William Amerman.)

A photograph of Ann Stovall Field, with Earl Skillman's race car, in May 1930. The North Branch Church can be seen in the background. (Field family.)

A c. 1934 photograph of Carl Blaufuss in his 1913 Ford, with his dog Laddie on the hood and a friend, Frank or George Runyon, in the passenger's seat (chin on hand). Carl was born in the house at the corner of River Road and Mill Lane in 1917. (Wilma Farley Blaufuss.)

Francis Geisinger courting Joanna Little on his Indian motorcycle with side car in 1917. They were married the next year, a marriage that was to last over fifty years. The photograph was taken in front of her family house, on Lamington Road, which now belongs to the Raritan Valley Community College (see p. 22). (Robert Van Pelt, *A Genealogy of the Little Family*, 1992.)

George Field plowing the roads during the great snow storm of 1924–25. (Field family.)

An outing in the country July 6, 1927. George Field is at the wheel, with Frank Lane beside him. In the back seat are Mrs. Frank Lane, Mrs. Hageman, and Alice Field, behind her husband George. George Field owned the creamery and lumber yard at North Branch Depot. Frank Lane ran the lumber yard for him. (Field family.)

The 1923 Lumberman's Convention in New York City. George Field (fourth row from the left, with his elbow on the seat) owned the lumber yard at North Branch Depot (now the Printmaker's Council). (Field family.)

Always an upscale community, this round five-door, five-hole outhouse must have made the neighbors jealous. No waiting! Located behind a house on Old Turnpike Road, it survived until a couple of years ago when it fell to development. (Branchburg Historic Preservation Commission.)

The Studdiford family reunion, Labor Day, 1924. The lion on the right, one of two which flanked the entrance to Bill Bradley's estate at Bradley Gardens, is now in the possession of Grace Staats. This house is today the home of the Kanach family, "River Lea Farm," on South Branch Road. (Walter Studdiford.)

Running for reelection in the early 1940s is Paul Farley (right), who was overseer of the poor for twenty-five years on the township committee from 1939 to 1956, and mayor for three consecutive terms. The other men are, from left to right, William Higgins (who was tax accessor and who owned the farm at the corner of Readington Road and Route 22), Frank Lane (who owned the farm from Station Road to the railroad tracks on Readington Road), and William Vanderbeek. (Lee Hamilton.)

The wedding of Wilma Farley and Carl Blaufuss at the North Branch Reformed Church, November 2, 1941. The wedding party, from left to right, are: (front row) Edith (Nuss) Bergen, Milda (Robinson) Dumont, Wilma Farley (the bride), Kathryn (Dumont) Greenaway, and Faith Farley (the flower girl, age five); (back row) James Farley, Arthur Stillwell, Edward Blaufuss (the best man), Carl Blaufuss (the groom), Robert Dumont, and James Vanderveer. (Wilma Farley Blaufuss.)